1

To Dawn

from Erma Nixon

A WALK WITH ERNA NIXON

Dawn Flybirdie Hawks

Prologue

This is a love letter. It is with great love and gratitude I come to write this book. The founders of Melbourne Village had such vision. They came to share their knowledge without hesitation; encouraging one another, contributing what gifts they had to make a healthy community. One was Erna Nixon. She was a teacher, a Quaker/Friend by faith, a missionary to Jamaica, and a trained concert pianist. She never had children. She came to teach three or four children in Melbourne Village of nature. Singularly she took us to walk with her weekly. What she did teach beyond scientific fact was a love and appreciation for all things. I hope by sharing these words you will come to better see.

Hammock is a term used in the southeastern United States for stands of trees, usually hardwood, that form an ecological island in a contrasting ecosystem. Hammocks grow on elevated areas, often just a few inches high, surrounded by wetlands that are too wet to support them. Hammocks are also often classified as hydric (wet soil), mesic (moist soil) or xeric (dry soil). The types are not exclusive, but often grade into each other.

Keystone species is a term used when an animal provides an environ that helps other species have homes. They play a critical role in maintaining the structure of an ecological community, affecting many other organisms in an ecosystem and helping to determine the types and numbers of various other species in the community. The word keystone comes from an architectural term dealing with the construction of a building, meaning that if one key part were removed the whole building would tumble down.

Ecosystem this term is used to describe a
biological community of interacting organisms and
their physical environment.

I grew up in the southern wood, Pollywogs on my
toes, Crawdaddies, Black Mollies, and Guppies in
the water. There were Luna moths, Flying Squirrel,
Whip Poor Wills, Cicadas buzzing in the trees,
even Bumbley Bees! Eastern Meadowlark in
every field, O jubilant their cry!
Great Blue Heron, Snowy Egret, Ibis flying by!

Painted Box turtle, Snappers too, Gopher tortoise
walking slowly, Oh my! Black Racer, Diamond
Back, Garden, King, and Coral snake. I was
careful, make no mistake. Black Bear and Panther
prowling. Wild Rabbit, Fox, Opossum, and
Racoon; some travel by day others by the moon.

Walking Sticks, Velvet Ants, Beetles, and Potters
Wasps, always insects to bemuse without cost.
Guava, Fern, Bromeliad, Pine, Oak, every shape
and texture. My teacher talked softly and she need
not lecture. I loved it then!
O to go on walks with Erna Nixon; who with great
reverence, taught me appreciation of all things.
She spoke to me in a way that I, as a child, could

understand. All the world was beauteous wonder. O the land was interesting, so much to see and hear.

I met Erna Nixon when I was 11, her weekly walks with me in the Hammock would impact my entire life.

Come with me then, on a walk with Erna Nixon.

I would walk through Deer Head Hammock to approach Erna's door. The morning was often warm and bright. Dewdrops sparkled on spider webs. Wild rabbits hopped by. I often stopped to lift fern's leaves to look at the cinnamon colored spore cases beneath. I liked the pattern and contrasting color. I walked atop oak leaves. As they decayed they added to the richness of earth's essence. The morning smelled wonderful.

"Knock, knock."

The screen door opened. Erna's lovely smile greeted me. "Hello bright eyes," she'd always say, "Come in." I would enter in to her living room full of books. We would sit in silence before we entered in to the hammock. In retrospect, I understand, she was waiting. For I have come to know, in silence much is heard. Selah, pause and realize.

(*The practice of sitting together in silence is often called "expectant waiting." It is a time when Friends become inwardly still and clear aside*

the activities of mind and body that usually fill our attention to create an opportunity to experience the presence of the Holy Spirit. It is not a time for "thinking," for deliberate, intellectual exercise. It is a time for spiritual receptivity, so it is important not to clog one's mind with its own busy activities and to become centered.)

In given time, we would arise to go walking. As we approached the hammock, rays of light streamed through the branches.

Long Wing
Zebra
Butterfly

If we went very early in the morning, we might spy Zebra Butterflies roosting on a few branches of a shrub. Zebra Butterfly adults roost communally at night in groups of up to 60 adults for safety from predators. They gather in roosts to spend the night returning to the same place daily. Therefore, we knew where to look. When roosting, the oldest ones choose the best places. They also gently nudge the others early in the morning to get going. It was fun to watch them arise. They would fly slowly and gracefully away.

An unusual feature of the longwing zebra butterflies; the adults are relatively long lived. Most other butterflies live only a few weeks, but zebra butterflies continue to live and to lay eggs for several months. Their tropical or semitropical habitat makes this possible; furthermore, the feeding habits of the adults are important in prolonging their lives. The adults feed on nectar of flowers, like most other butterflies, but they also feed on pollen. Most butterflies can only sip fluids with their specialized mouth parts, but the butterflies take some pollen as well as nectar. Pollen is very nutritious, rich in proteins, unlike nectar which contains almost no proteins, just sugars. This diet allows the butterflies to prolong their lives and enables them to continue producing eggs for several months. They are more dependent on flowers than other types of butterflies and this makes them good pollinators. Some of their favorites are lantana and shepherd's needle. Oh, do not rub against the plant of shepherd's needle, for you 'll be picking sharp long seeds from your clothes or socks!

Beauty Berry

We would enter in to the canopy's umbrella of trees. Purple Beautyberries and Marlberry added color.

Beautyberry occurs naturally over a wide portion of the southeastern United States. It is highly tolerant of a variety of conditions. It likes to pop up at the forest edges where it gets plenty of light with a bit of shade.it is very drought tolerant, but does need good drainage. It reaches heights of 5 to 9 feet, frequently as wide as it is high. The natural shape is something of a mound form with gracefully arching branches. Beautyberries have delicate flowers, drought resistance and value to wildlife. The berries, which you may see at almost any time of year, are magenta swirls of tightly clustered little globes.

Marlberry

Marlberry is a 12- to 15-foot-tall shrub. It often occurs naturally with Sabal Palms. The dark green, semi glossy leaves of this shrub are 3 to 4 ½ inches long. The small, white, fragrant flowers occur in dense clusters 5 inches in length. Flowers are borne at intervals throughout the year but do not last very long. In the late spring this plant bears its small purple fruit. Marlberry is a super wildlife supporter. It not only provides food and nectar for a wide variety of animals, birds, and butterflies, but it is dense enough to provide good cover, too.

The Seminoles used Marlberry wood to make arrows, as skewers to roast meats, and ate the berries for food. They also used the leaves as an "extender" for their smoking tobacco.

Brachen Fern

Bracken ferns covered the forest floor. *Bracken fern is a perennial fern occurring in dry to wet forests, meadows, clearings, sandy soils, roadsides, lake-shores, and bogs; in both older forests and in new pine forests, especially those frequently burned. It is also found in abandoned pastures and along forest margins. The underground stems or rhizomes are deep, giving it the ability to survive intense fires. Bracken fern is found in acid soils. Bracken fern has stiff, upright, branching fronds that grow from creeping and forking underground rhizomes. It grows up to 4½' tall and has triangular-shaped fronds. Wind disperses the spores usually after a fire or disturbance. This fern does not grow in clusters as many ferns do. The bracken fern also provides minor amounts of cover for wildlife.*

Native Americans used the rhizomes as food. They roasted the dried rhizomes in an open fire, broke the rhizomes into pieces and ate them or steamed the rhizomes in pits or made a type of bread.

Golden Orb Weaver

Often, a Golden Orb Spider (locally called Banana spider), would have woven a huge 3-foot web across the path. We would stop to investigate. What had the spider caught in its web? We would closely look, was there a fly, a moth, a beetle, dragon fly, mosquito, or a wasp? Many different flying insects could be encased in silk. Mummies on golden silk spider webs! Was the spider male or female? The larger is always a female. Before we passed, she did a very thoughtful thing.

"Now let's be careful, this web so beautiful of design, took the spider a long time to make." She took one of the anchor lines and moved it aside. We would then pass under the web without disturbing it. Then she'd return the anchor line ever carefully. And in her tutelage with others, she showed by action, how to touch the earth gently. Replacing the anchor line just where we had removed it, we would walk deeper in to the hammock.

Onward we'd walk under Cabbage Palms, some had Bromeliad, or Fern in their trunk brackets.

Golden Polypody

Golden Polypody is strongly associated with Florida's state tree, the Cabbage Palm (Sabal palmetto). The roots and spreading rhizome of this fern grow in the nooks of Cabbage Palm boots, the broken leaf stems that project outward from the trunk. The fern's rhizome, a modified stem, can snake its way down the cabbage palm trunk and send up new leaves. This habit is what gave rise to the strange name "polypody," which means "many feet." Some people refer to this plant as a

Rabbit's Foot Fern because its rhizome is covered with soft, hair like scales that invite a gentle touch from passersby. The scales are a warm amber color, which has also led to another common name Gold Foot Fern.

"Oh, look," she'd exclaim, "The palms are like messy children tossing their clothes on the floor". Palms drop their fronds to allow for moisture to be held near the tree's root ball. Also, many species find refuge beneath the fronds. We would look by lifting a frond. "Today what to find? A salamander, a snake, wood roach, beetle, ants, millipedes, spiders, sow bugs, centipedes hmm? Someone is busy at work."

Millipedes consume leaf litter. After digesting, they drop fecal pellets. Bacteria and fungi eat these pellets. This adds to soil nourishment. Other arthropods eat the pellets and this also adds to the soil; nature building soil like a compost system. An interesting feature of millipedes is that they have moisture beads on their exoskeleton. The moisture contains iodine and this deters predators.

Salamanders are fond of rolled petioles of palm fronds. The salamander's diet are insects, spiders, and worms. Smaller salamanders often feed on beetles and their larvae, flies, earthworms, moths, grasshoppers, mites, and springtails.

It was always fun to see who we would find. We would observe awhile, then replace the frond. Erna told me another thing special about palm fronds, the old dead ones clinging yet to the tree provided nice roosting perch for bats!

Northern Yellow Bat

Florida's native bats are insectivorous; meaning they eat insects including beetles, mosquitoes, moths, and other agriculture and garden pests.

Bats live in many different habitats across Florida. They can be found in dry, upland pine forests, in the hardwood forests along the banks of rivers, and most habitats in-between. For bats, one of the most important parts of their habitat is a place to roost. In Florida, natural roosting sites can be caves, in cracks, crevices, or hollows of trees, under dead fronds of palm trees, and in Spanish moss.

Bats also use manmade structures including buildings, bridges, culverts, tile roofs, and bat houses. The following may be found in the hammock.

Seminole Bat

The fur of the Seminole Bat is a rich mahogany color. On some individuals, the tips of the fur are white, giving them a slightly frosted appearance. A patch of white fur is often found on the shoulders and wrists. Seminole Bats are closely related to the Eastern Red Bat and are very similar in appearance. Their wingspan is 11-13 inches, body length 1.8-2.7 inches, and they weigh 0.3-0.5 ounces.

They roost alone, commonly found in pine trees and Spanish moss. They feed on moths, beetles, true bugs, flies, and other insects.

Eastern Red Bat

The fur of male Eastern Red Bats is usually brick-red in color, but can be reddish-orange or yellowish-red. The fur of female Red Bats is duller and lighter in color. This is unusual because color differences between male and female bats is rare. A patch of white fur is often found on the shoulders and wrists. The Eastern Red Bat and the Seminole Bat are closely related, and similar in appearance, but the fur of the Seminole Bat is more mahogany in color, and there are no color differences between male and female Seminole Bats. Their wingspan is 11-13 inches, body length 2.0-2.4 inches, and weighs 0.3-0.5 ounces.

They roost alone in tree foliage or bushes. They usually hang from small branches or twigs, and appear much like a dead leaf. They feed on moths, beetles, mosquitoes, leafhoppers, planthoppers, flies, and other insects. Although they capture most of their prey in the air, they have occasionally been observed gleaning insects from objects and the ground.

Northern Yellow Bat

*The Northern Yellow Bat is one of Florida's larger bat species. Its long, thick fur varies in color from yellowish- to grayish-brown. This enables it to be well camouflaged in its preferred roost habitat of dead palm fronds. Their wingspan is 14-16 inches, body length 2.8-2.8 inches. They roost alone primarily in the dead palm fronds of sabal palms, but occasionally roosts in Spanish moss. **The practice of trimming dead palm fronds in urban areas destroys habitat for this species**. They feed on beetles, flies, damselflies, leafhoppers, flying ants, and other insects.*

Evening bat

The fur of the Evening bat is usually a dark brown, but may also have a bronze to reddish tint. It has short dark ears and the muzzle is broad, unfurred, and nearly black. This species closely resembles the big brown bat, but is smaller in size. Their wingspan is 10-11 inches, body length is 1.9-2.6 inches, weight 0.2-0.4 ounces.

They roost in colonies. Colony sizes range from just a few to around seventy or so bats. They roost behind loose bark and the crevices and cavities of dead trees. On a few occasions, they have been found in Spanish moss. They feed on beetles, planthoppers, true bugs, flies, mosquitoes, moths, flying termites, flying ants, and other insects.

Southeastern Myotis

The fur of the Southeastern Myotis varies in color from brown to gray, to brownish-orange. The individual hairs are bicolored with the lower portion being darker than the tips. Their wingspan is 9-11 inches, body length 1.9-2.1 inches and weight 0.2-0.3 ounces. They roost in colonies. The Southeastern Myotis is primarily a cave dwelling species, but also roosts in hollow trees. Mosquitoes make up a significant portion of the diet of the Southeastern Myotis, but they also fed on moths, beetles, crane flies, and other insects. They typically forage over ponds, streams, lakes, and rivers near the water's surface.

Bromeliad
and Ruby Throated Hummingbird

We would come to also identify bromeliads.
Which were blooming? Cardinal Bromeliad has a
beautiful violet bloom, Twisted Air Plant has rose
or purple, a Potbelly Bromeliad has a lavender

flower.

Bromeliads are related to the pineapple family. Their thick, waxy leaves form a bowl shape in the center for catching rainwater. Some bromeliads can hold several gallons of water and are miniature ecosystems in themselves providing homes for several creatures including frogs and their tadpoles, salamanders, snails, beetle, and mosquito larvae. Those that die decompose and furnish the plant with nutrients. One may find bromeliads to contain beetles, crane flies, earwigs, frog, cockroach, spiders, fly larvae, millipede, scorpion, woodlice, or an earthworm!

Further along the path a palm tree had fallen over. It snaked along the ground, then reached up for light again. There we'd look to see how recent the panther's scratches were on the trunk. Erna would touch the claw marks and remark, "This is the panthers address mark."

Florida Panther

Panthers hone their claws by scratching on logs or trees. These scratches are probably not a form of territory marking or communication to other panthers, but they do alert humans to the presence of panthers. In Florida, the preferred "scratching post" seems to be fallen down cabbage palms with smooth trunks.

Sadly, I saw hanging over Evan's Grove/Ranch, where the huge Melbourne Mall now sits, a large dead panther with its beautiful huge paws and tawny fur. I often thought it had been the very one that wandered in the hammock. For shortly after fresh marks were nary seen again.

Pileated Woodpecker

The path took a bend around the fallen palm as we walked deeper into the hammock, we'd often hear a pileated woodpecker. "Oh, listen to him laugh," Erna would say.

The largest of our woodpeckers is a wonder to see with its red crest and black and white feathers. The Pileated Woodpecker is a keystone species. Their old nest (which is easy to identify as they are squared off), and roost cavities provide unique habitat for secondary cavity-users. Their drilling holes provide foraging opportunities for other species, quicken decay processes, and control insect outbreaks.

When abandoned, these holes—made similarly by all woodpeckers—provide good homes in future years for many forest song birds and a wide variety of other animals. Owls and tree-nesting ducks may largely rely on holes made by Pileated Woodpeckers in which to lay their nests. Even mammals such as raccoons may use them. Other woodpeckers and smaller birds such as wrens may be attracted to pileated holes to feed on the insects found in them. Ecologically, the entire woodpecker family is important to the wellbeing of many other bird species.

Deeper we would wander, green surrounded us, seemingly taking us far removed from the busy streets of the work a day world nearby.

Wild Coffee

We would admire wild coffee with its beautiful berries, and ferns in the understory of oak.

Wild coffee is found in the higher areas of swamps and in hydric and mesic hammocks and areas that are seasonally wet and dry.

Wild coffee is so named not because it is a coffee substitute but because the fruits resemble those of the common coffee shrub; the fruit is an oval drupe that matures red, to scarlet to maroon. The drupes measure on average 5/16 inches in diameter and contains 2 seeds. A variety of birds eat the fruit including the Florida state bird the Northern Mockingbird, Blue Jays, Cardinals, and Catbirds through Summer and Autumn.

On towards the largest Live Oak in the hammock, with far reaching canopy. Oh, to look up and stand in awe, and realize this tree had hosted many species for hundreds of years! Often a Great Horned Owl was seen one of the great branches. Every branch was covered with resurrection fern, with our high humidity, or if it had rained, they would perk up. Orchids also blossomed.

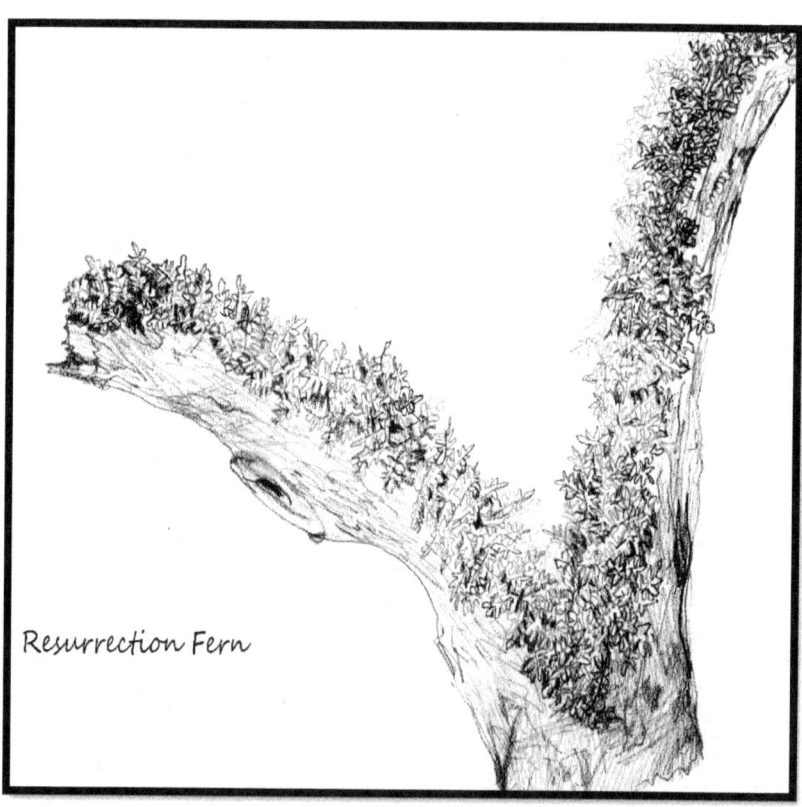

Resurrection Fern

Resurrection fern is a remarkable plant. It can lose about 75 percent of its water content during a typical dry period and possibly up to 97 percent in an extreme drought. During this time, it shrivels up to a grayish brown clump of leaves. When it is exposed to water again, it will "come back to life" and look green and healthy. The plant gets its name from this supposed "resurrection," but it never actually dies during the process. By contrast, most other plants can only lose 10 percent of their water content before they die. Fronds are typically 4 to 12 inches in length. Due to its ability to withstand drought, it can be found in variety of habitats, but it needs a host plant or other substrate on which to anchor. Resurrection Fern often favors oak trees. The Resurrection Fern is a type of epiphytic fern. (It grows on top of other plants or structures.)

Tupelo

Tupelo grew in low areas near the marsh. We would stand below the huge tupelo and if blossoming, we could hear a hum of bees. We might also see butterflies and birds.

The tupelo tree is an important food source for many migrating birds in the autumn. Its early color change is thought to attract birds to the available fruit, which ripen before many other fall fruits and berries. The fruit is quite marked, dark blue, in clusters of two or three. Many kinds of birds eagerly seek the sour fruits, including: American Robin, Hermit Thrush, Wood Thrush, Cardinal, Mockingbird, Blue Jay, Red-Bellied Woodpecker, Yellow-Bellied Sapsucker, Pileated Woodpecker, Eastern Phoebe, Brown Thrasher, Scarlet Tanager, Gray Catbird, and American Crow, all primarily eastern North American birds migrating or residing year-round within the tree's range. A Tupelo may grow to be 66–82 ft. tall, rarely 115 ft., with a trunk diameter of 20–39 in, rarely up 67 in. These trees typically have a straight trunk with the branches extending outward at right angles. The bark is dark gray and flaky when young, but it becomes furrowed with age, resembling alligator hide on very old stems.

Mulberry

We would come to stand beneath the Mulberry tree, so tall, 50 to 70 feet, with a beautiful canopy. "O listen. Who do we hear?", Erna said to me.

Many species of birds and small mammals eat the fruits of Mulberry. Birds that enjoy Mulberries are; Wood Ducks, Bluebirds, Indigo Buntings, Gray Catbirds, Eastern Kingbirds, Towhees, Brown Thrashers, Tanagers, Vireos, Red-Cockaded Woodpeckers (rare to see as they are endangered by habitat loss), and Great Crested Flycatchers. Mammals that visited the tree would include opossums, raccoons, and gray squirrels. White-tailed deer browse the twigs and foliage.

Opossum

Dahoon Holly

In the understory, we'd find Dahoon Holly. When in flower we'd see butterfly and birds.

Dahoon Holly is usually found in moist to wet locations and wetland thickets. Small to medium or rarely a large tree with variable crowns composed of numerous branches. Trunks are often short, branching near the ground, 6-12 inches in diameter. Bark whitish to grayish to almost black, often covered with numerous lichens and other epiphytes (air plants). The smooth, shiny dark green, evergreen leaves, two to three inches long, have just a few serrations near the tip. The flowers are white, cream, or grey. They possess male and female flowers on separate plants. The berries are round, small, and yellow/ red. The fruit is an excellent food source for wildlife; and attracts squirrels, small mammals, red-eyed vireos, and other songbirds. Deer browse the young growth.

The sloping path opened to the marshy pond, there we'd see Buttonbush and Dragonflies.

"O look, how they fly on such marvelous wings."

I loved watching them perch on reeds. I then would study their eyes, body, and yes, their cellophane like wings. Arial wonders they are!

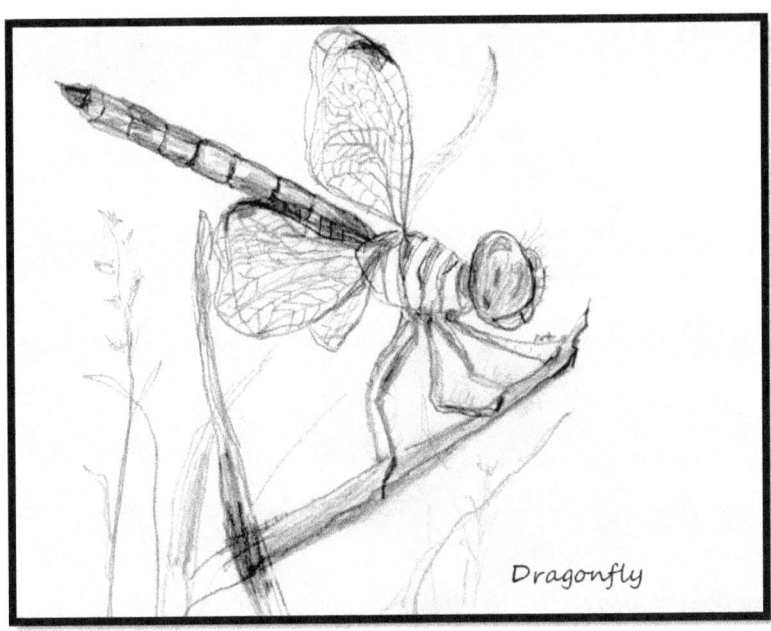

Dragonfly

Dragonflies are extremely important in indicating the health of ecosystems, and overall environmental quality. Dragonflies are one of nature's many precious species giving us a physical sense of our damage or care of water.

Spending most of their lives underwater in rivers, streams, ponds, lakes, their presence in aquatic environments will signify water quality as dragonflies and damselflies require clean water to thrive. Their survival also requires healthy native vegetation to provide oxygen and clean the water. Vegetation also aids them to hide and for their transformation process from nymphs to adult fliers. If dragonflies are absent from or near a body of water, the potential issues may be pesticides and excessive nutrients from agricultural landscapes, siltation from soil and bank erosion, various water contaminants from human settlement, and industry or urban landscapes.

Dragonflies are also beneficial to potential human health risks by consuming mosquitoes and their larvae. They also eat a range of other insect life at various metamorphic phases. Damselflies are their close relatives but differ in that the dragonfly's forewings differ from their hind ones and both sets remain open at rest unlike the damselfly. The larval stage of the dragonfly is spent underwater and eaten by frogs, fish, newts, and other invertebrates.

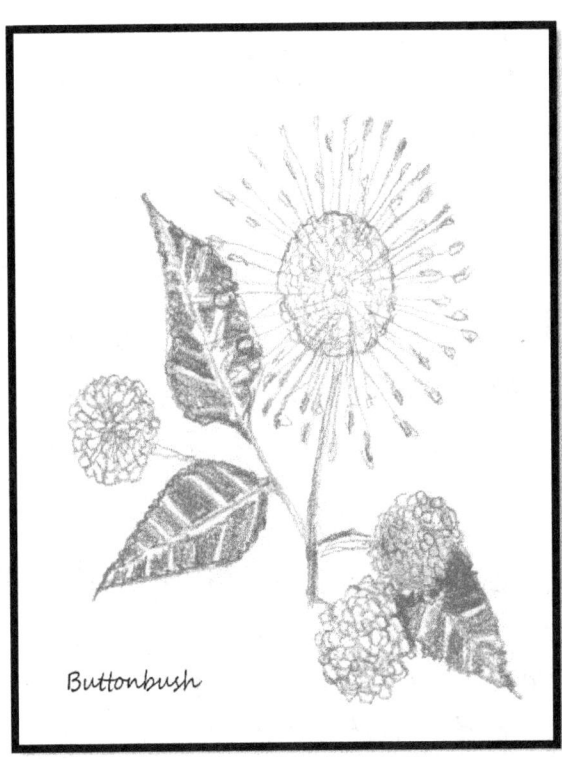

Buttonbush

Buttonbush grows naturally in freshwater wet-
lands at the margins of swamps and pond.
Buttonbush can be a pioneer species in frequently
flooded swamps by establishing itself on rotting
logs and stumps. The buttonbush shrub can grow
to become a small tree but usually does not attain
a height of more than 10 to 12 feet. This multi-
stemmed, rounded bush has arching branches and

a somewhat open and spreading appearance. The coarse stems are almost 4-sided. Stem color varies from gray-brown to shiny olive, turning reddish-brown with age. The bark is smooth, becoming ridged and furrowed, often with vertical, raised, corky lenticels (one of many raised pores in the stem of a woody plant that allows gas exchange between the atmosphere and the internal tissues.) These 1-1½" flower spheres are on long pedicels, (a stem that attaches a single flower to the inflorescence.) The flowers have a star like inflorescence;(the complete flower head of a plant including stems, stalks, bracts, and flowers). And has many white stamens extending beyond the corollas and topped by yellow anthers.

The Buttonbush shrubs can form colonies from self-sown seedlings and root sprouts. The plant has a scrubby appearance due to the dying of leader shoots, which leave dead and dying stumps. The flowers attract butterflies, bees, and hummingbirds. The seeds are a food source for ducks. The ducks also use the plant for shelter. For humans, it is highly toxic.

Fern stood in large clumps on the shore's edge or on old stumps. There were Cinnamon, Royal, Swamp, and Strap Ferns.

.Cinnamon Fern

Cinnamon Fern occurs in moist, boggy ground along streams and on shaded areas near ponds. Typically grows in clumps to 2-3' tall. Separate spore-bearing, stiff, fertile fronds appear in early spring, quickly turning brown. It is a deciduous plant which produces separate fertile and sterile fronds. The sterile fronds are spreading, to 5 ft.

tall and 5 to 7 in. broad. The fertile spore-bearing fronds are erect and shorter, 8in to 18 in. tall; they become cinnamon-colored, which gives the species its name. The fertile leaves appear first; their green color slowly becomes brown as the season progresses and the spores are dropped. The Cinnamon Fern forms huge colonies in swampy areas. These ferns form massive rootstocks with densely matted, wiry roots. Fuzz which covers the young fiddleheads is a favorite nesting material for birds. Cinnamon Ferns do not actually produce cinnamon; they are named for the color of the fronds.

Royal Fern

Royal Fern is a large and dramatic fern that grows from a stout rhizome which creeps along the ground, then ascends like a stump to give rise to a crown-shaped tussock of light green leaves. The rootstock, with its mass of wiry black fibers, can be as much as 12 in. above the soil line. Most kinds of ferns bear their reproductive spores on the underside of their leaves, but the Osmunda ferns have their spores in clusters on specialized fronds. The whole leaf can be up to 6 ft. long, and looks more like mimosa, locust, or acacia than a typical fern. Royal Fern is the largest and most spectacular fern occurring in North America. This is one of the most common ferns found throughout much of Florida.

The Cinnamon Fern and Royal Fern are listed by The Florida Department of Agriculture as a "Commercially Exploited Species," which means that it cannot be removed from the wild for commercial purposes without a permit.

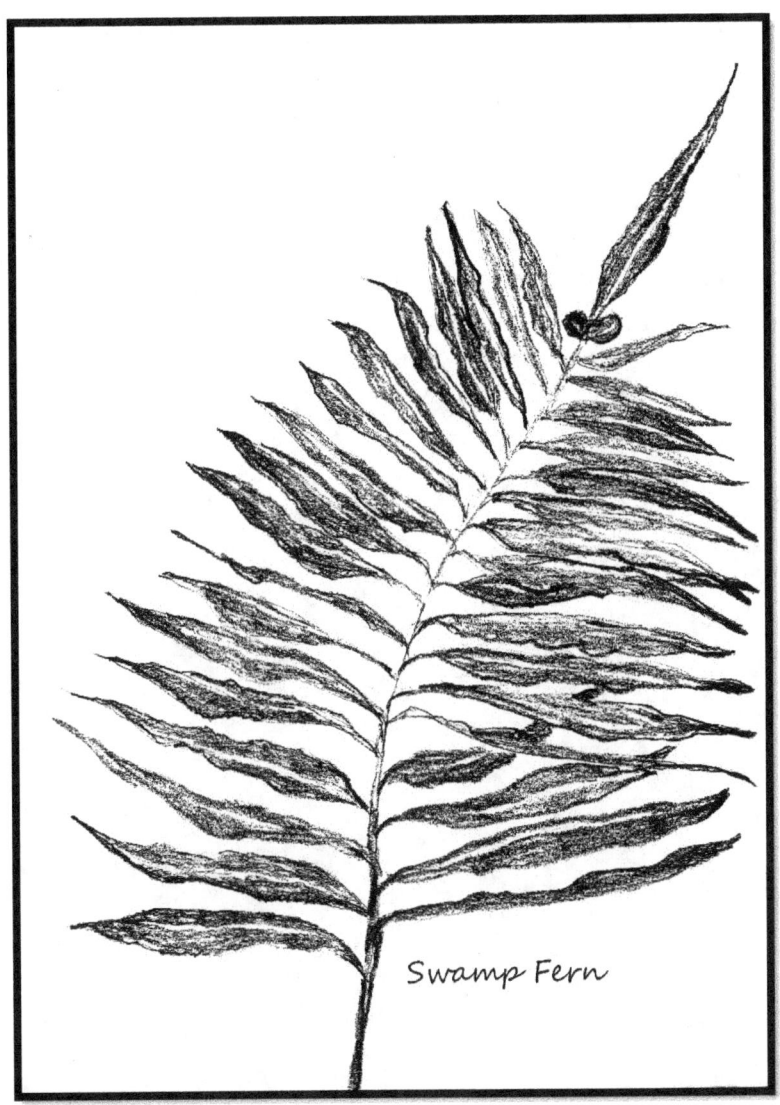

Swamp Fern

Swamp Fern is found in large moist sites at the edges of ponds, swamps, and marshes. It is an upright fern capable of growing to 4 feet in height. The fronds are pinnate with a single, apical leaflet.

The leaflets are crinkled with serrated edges. The new growth is coppery pink in color becoming dark green. The fronds grow shorter and leatherier in the sun and taller and more pliable in shade but they grow readily in either condition. The Swamp Fern easily spreads into areas that support its growth.

Strap Fern

Long Strap Fern needs a little something to hold on to. A rock, a stump, or a decaying log will do. Long strap fern is an epiphyte.

The long, leathery, yellow-green fronds make it easy to identify. The leaves are straight, with a slight wave along the edges. It will grow to two or three feet tall, a little narrower than it is high. Some of the fronds are marked on one side with rows of yellowish dots which produce spores that spread the plant. Long strap fern is found in moist, shady places, including cypress swamps and hammocks. It also can be found growing on the walls of limestone sinkholes.

Nesting Ruby-Throated
Hummingbird

I loved seeing hummingbirds; both coral bean, and bromeliads blossoming attracted them. Once by watching closely, we found where a hummingbird's nest was located.

The Ruby-Throated hummingbird is by far the most common hummingbird in the state. This feathered jewel is about 3 inches long and weighs as little as a penny. Its name describes the most brilliant part of the mature male's plumage. The throat feathers contain air bubbles that give off an iridescent red tone in full light. Their backs are metallic green.

Centuries ago their plumage was used to adorn Native American ceremonial costumes.

Although some birds may stay in south Florida year-round, most winter in Mexico and South America. Males arrive in Florida in March. Females arrive about a week later.

Nesting in Florida begins in April. The nest is a walnut-size structure of plant down, adorned with lichens, moss, and bound with spider webs or fine plant fibers. Nests frequently are built over water. The female lays 2 eggs less than ½ inch long. After 20 days of incubation and 4 weeks of growing, young hummingbirds leave the nest.

Hummingbirds do not hum; their rapid wing movements (50–200 beats per second) make sound. Hummingbirds need to consume large amounts of high-energy food. Adult hummingbirds feed primarily on nectar. Young are fed insects by their parents, but are switched to a mostly nectar diet by the time they leave the nest. One hummingbird may need nectar from hundreds of blossoms every day to maintain its body weight. They also feed to a lesser extent on insects. For their size, hummingbirds have among the largest appetites in the bird world. They feed every 10 or 15 minutes from dawn until dusk. During this period, they eat more than half their weight in food and 8 times their weight in water. Hummingbirds have developed 2 adaptations to help them survive the hours of darkness when they cannot feed. First, they eat as much as they can just before dark. During the night, their heart rate and body temperature drop to conserve energy. If they did not go into this sort of daily hibernation stage (torpor), they likely would starve.

Fox Grape

Fox grape draped, climbed, and hung off trees. I nibbled grapes off hanging vines. Yum. I wondered what others did also?

On a Cabbage Palm, we would look at a clinging
Shoestring Fern. "Is it going to rain today Dawn?"

When one looks at how far a Shoestring Fern is
sticking out from the palm, if it clings it will be
very dry. If full it is going to be moist.

Shoestring Fern

*Shoestring Fern's preferred habitat is moist
woods; palms, as noted, are a favorite place to
grow, although it will find a home on other trees*

as well. The fronds are dark green, narrow, and long, and a foot-and-a-half or more. The undersides have two groove-like strips where spores form. Shoestring fern grows in light to moderate shade but does not tolerate drought well. Common names for shoestring fern include ribbon fern and grass fern.

Beyond the deep hammock land, in the dry xeric area past the marshy pond, we would see gopher tortoise grazing on wiregrass. One might easily walk right by one if not carefully observing, as they are quiet.

They are now a protected species. They are a keystone species. The gopher tortoise burrows are especially important because the burrows dug by the tortoise can provide homes for many other animals.

This is called commensal living, a place where other animals can live and raise their young. Juvenile tortoises, the Florida mouse, lizards, diamondback rattlesnakes, and toads all spend time in the burrow. The burrow sometimes up to fifty plus feet, also provides a home for larger mammals, rabbits, armadillos, skunks, opossums, and foxes. Even the scrub jay and burrowing owl spend time below ground. The endangered indigo snake also relies on the burrow for its offspring. The gopher frog, gopher scarab beetle, gopher cricket, and the gopher moth, are rarely found anywhere but in the burrows that the tortoise digs. Many invertebrates such as worms, scorpions, spiders, ticks, and flies also inhabit the burrow. Ants and beetles are probably the most common.

As many as 360 species visit the burrow at one time or another. These animals do not harm the tortoise. In fact, the tortoise doesn't seem to mind the guests.
The gopher tortoise provides the burrow for a variety of animals, to live different lifestyles in the same location.
When the burrow is currently a home of a gopher tortoise, it will have a half moon shaped opening. It will be clean of debris and have a sandy

entrance. After a gopher tortoise has abandoned a burrow; other animals like owls, armadillos, or fox may occupy the burrow. The opening will be round and not as clean.

Some of their favorite foods in the hammock are stinging nettle, lantana, poison ivy, beautyberry, and wiregrass. A basic in the diet of the gopher tortoise is the many varieties of grass.

Florida Native Wiregrass, also called Pineland Threeawn, is one of the most common grasses in the southern pine flatwoods and upland sand hills. It is a favorite food of gopher tortoises and quail; and provides valuable cover for many birds, reptiles, and small mammals. Wiregrass is a perennial bunch grass that grows in dense, spreading tufts, reaching heights of 1½' to 3'. The leaves are long, thin, wiry, or needle-like with tufts of fine, white fuzz around the leaf base.

Bobcat

Elusive, yet we saw rare glimpses of the Florida Bobcat! O how we would smile.

One can easily identify the Florida Bobcat by its short tail (or bob) and the fringes of fur that outline the sides of its head. Their ears are pointed with short, black tufts. They weigh between 13 and 30 pounds and have a tail with white on its underside and black markings on its top side. The Bobcat has spots of white on all parts of its fur, which can range in color from reddish-brown to grey. The adult Bobcat can grow to about 50 inches in length and stands 21 inches tall on average. With a maximum adult weight of 35 pounds, the bobcat is similar in size to a young Florida panther for which it is sometimes mistaken. Bobcats are about twice the size of a domestic cat.

Widely distributed throughout Florida in deep forest, swamps, and hammock land. Thick patches of saw palmetto and dense shrub thickets are important as den and resting sites. In rural areas, Bobcats can range five or six square miles and generally cover their territory in a slow, careful fashion. In urban to suburban areas, the range of territory usually decreases to 1 or 2 miles.

An efficient hunter, the bobcat hunts by sight and usually at night. Seeing a Bobcat during the day is not rare, because they sleep for only 2 to 3 hours at a time. Squirrels, rabbits, and rats are the primary prey species. Occasionally, a Bobcat will take a feral cat or domestic chicken. Since Florida is an important wintering area for migrating birds, the Bobcat's winter diet reflects this abundance and includes ground-dwelling birds such as *towhees, robins, catbirds, and thrashers.*

In the humus, rich moist soil areas of the hammock we were fortunate to find Jack in the Pulpit, and Erna would say, "What do you think he what he might be preaching about?"

I now believe,

Jack in the Pulpit doth say, "Let us pray. Let us walk gently and have reverence for all about. The earth sustains us and all has reason to be. Tenderly, come to understand and see, the land, the waters, the many species all work together. We are but a part of the whole and we have responsibility to be good stewards."

And so, as I came to visit Erna after she had
suffered a stroke, I brought a poetry book, to read.
She had not spoken since her stroke, just nodded
her head to answer. I asked if she would like to
hear the poem,

"The Road Not Taken, by Robert Frost?"

She enthusiastically nodded yes and then I began,

"Two roads diverged in a yellow wood,

And sorry I could not travel both

And be one traveler, long I stood

And looked down one as far as I could

To where it bent in the undergrowth;

Then took the other, as just as fair,

And having perhaps the better claim,

Because it was grassy and wanted wear;

Though as for that the passing there

Had worn them really about the same,

And both that morning equally lay

In leaves no step had trodden black.

Oh, I kept the first for another day!

Yet knowing how way leads on to way,

I doubted if I should ever come back.

I shall be telling this with a sigh

Somewhere ages and ages hence:

Two roads diverged in a wood, and I—

I took the one less traveled by,

And that has made all the difference."

We both smiled. Here beside me was my mentor, my friend, a beautiful woman, Erna Emilie Nixon. She took the road less traveled by, and left a gift for others. In writing this I share the gift she bestowed upon me, a deep love for nature. May you receive the gift she helped preserve enjoying the hammock, Erna Nixon Park, Melbourne, Florida, USA.

From the dawn of time the earth revolves, the sun arises, and dew refreshes.

Birds, fish, amphibians, reptiles, insects, mammals, air, water, and land have come with purpose.

The value of our earth's resources is beyond monetary value.

We can choose to ignore, only visually enjoy, use, or **come to understand in the grand scheme how much we depend on one another.**

Birds you may see in different seasons:

CAROLINA WREN

CAROLINA CHICKADEE

NORTHERN CARDINAL

BLUE GREY GNATCATCHER

GREY CATBIRD

TUFTED TITMOUSE

AMERICAN REDSTART

BLUE JAY

MOURNING DOVE

NORTHERN MOCKING BIRD

WARBLERS

   YELLOW THROAT

   WORM EATTING

   YELLOW RUMPED

   PALM

RED EYED VIREOS

BLUE HEADED VIREOS

OVEN BIRDS

EASTERN PHOEBE

YELLOW BELLIED SAPSUCKER

RED HEADED WOODPECKER

PILEATED WOODPECKER

RED SHOULDERED HAWK

EASTERN SCREECH OWL

GREAT HORNED OWL

From the age of fifteen to nearly 30 years old, I had the privilege of knowing Erna.

Find forthwith a few correspondences, her memorial, and newspaper article.

Dear Dawn:

Thank you for your good letter. Always glad to hear from you.

I need a "Specialist" on Bromeliads. You are invited to be it! Congratulations on your "A". I think we have about 7 species in the Hammock, possibly 8. I found a short, dusty-pink one late last spring which I haven't identified as yet. It takes a surprising lot of time to check on some of our plants. The Botany teacher from Stetson U. told me yesterday that she still feels like a beginner.

There is a gate right near your lot which opens into the new park. The Park will be developed slowly, which is good for the plant-life. The work will go on only as the money comes in—no debts!

You will like the little lake called "Sunny Pond" at the north end of the Park.

Did I tell you that an excellent artist is making

sketches of plants in & near the hammock which will be printed up into a Coloring book for children? These books will be sold when the Administration Building is up. Everything takes time, however

I need to revise our plant-list. Perhaps you can help at that job. Several Botany classes from B.C.C. went thru our Trails recently

Did you know Steve Golder? He is now in Medical School at Gainesville. Next month he will be married in Deerhead Hammock. His bride lives in Jacksonville.

I am turning this note into a fair-sized letter, I see, and other matters are awaiting my attention. It may be this will have to serve as a Holiday greeting since my Christmas-list is long and time is getting shorter

So have a good Holiday beginning right now & on into 1975.

My love to all the Murpheys

Erna Nixon

Sunday
Nov. 10, 1974

May 24, 1974

Dear Sweet Graduate:

It just doesn't seem possible that your High School days are over!

My sincere congratulations and best wishes. I shall be much interested in the next step you take.

At long-last we are having our much needed rain, — for which we are grateful. This has been a very busy spring in the Hammock. Two groups of guests were from England, one from Scotland, and one made up of exchange students from Germany.

Thank you for sending the Commencement announcement. It is most attractive.

With love to all the Murpheys.

Erna Nixon

The wolf also shall dwell with the lamb, and the leopard shall lie down with the kid; and the calf and the young lion and the fatling together; and a little child shall lead them.

And the cow and the bear shall feed; their young ones shall lie down together; and the lion shall eat straw like the ox.

And the sucking child shall play on the hole of the asp, and the weaned child shall put his hand on the cockatrice's den.

They shall not hurt nor destroy in all my holy mountain; for the earth shall be full of the knowledge of the Lord, as the waters cover the sea.

ISAIAH XI: 6–9

ERNA NIXON WAS A LIFELONG MEMBER OF THE RELIGIOUS
SOCIETY OF FRIENDS. SHE WAS A RECORDED MINISTER.

William Penn, Friend, wrote in his Fruits of
Solitude, "Let us try what love will do--for if
others see we love them, we should find that they
would not harm us. Force may subdue, but love
gains; and he that forgives first, wins the laurel."

George Fox, 1624-1691, told us to "Walk cheer-
fully over the world, answering that of God in every-
one."

Erna exemplified these quotes--her gentle soul
respected, not only all people, but as all of us
gathered together know, flora and fauna, as well.

A memorial service for Friends is a meeting
for worship to celebrate the life of our Friend.
Those of us who are Friends are accustomed to
settling into the spirit of meditation as we approach our meeting place. We enter quietly, in
silence, take our seats, and commence to listen
to the "spirit" within us.

Today, we welcome you. One of our members
will share a biographical sketch, and then, we
will settle into our meeting for worship and
memories.

We hope that as any of you feel led, you will
contribute your thoughts from our silence, in the
manner of Friends--briefly. Do recognize, that the
meeting-as-a-whole continues to worship, each of
us in our own way. In approximately an hour, as the
meditation-level lifts, our clerk will end the
meeting by initiating the shaking of hands.

Today, we honor our memories of Erna Nixon,
knowing that she has affected each of us and that
our lives continue to be enriched for knowing her.

Erna Emilie Oesterreich Nixon

born

11-3-1891   Superior, Wisconsin

died

9-22-1985   Melbourne, Florida

Memorial Service

9-29-1985   2 P.M.
Melbourne Villiage Town Hall
Melbourne Villiage, Florida

Erna Nixon Hammock
provides a doorway
to the past . . . Page 3

Park preserves old-time Florida

By HUBERT GRIGGS

B   the little sentinel, Sunday, December 4, 1977   3

MELBOURNE — Civilization, internal combustion engines and hot asphalt pavements seem to slip away into some distant, yet-to-be time.

A few yards along the walkway leading into the Erna Nixon Hammock, just off Evans Road, the present seems to double back upon the past, and a stroller finds himself moving through timeless Florida pine woods.

The full impact of the hammock purchased in 1973 to preserve at least 52 acres of unspoiled native terrain, isn't felt, however, until the visitor moves or to the meandering boardwalk.

THE RUSTIC boardwalk dodges artfully through the hardwood and cabbage palm wilderness. Foreman Ed Jaques and his crew skillfully have guided the walkway and railings around trees, over fern beds and above the

rich mini-ecologies of fallen trees, to afford close views without leaving the boardwalk.

The boardwalk leads through the lush growth on a course that would be nearly impossible otherwise without hip boots. It allows close communion with fauna ranging from giant live oaks estimated at 400 years or more in age, through willows, palms, myrtles, elms, red maples and holly, past a rich variety of ferns and lichens, mosses and delicate air plants and butterfly orchids.

OCCASIONAL REST AREAS, equipped with benches, provide space for mini-lectures by guides, and an opportunity to pause, absorb the peace of the surroundings, and become aware of the activities of unobtrusive lizards, slow-moving gopher tortoises and the timid, armor-plated armadillos.

The initial 2,700 feet of boardwalk recently completed, departs from the county park's offi—utility meeting area pavilion, still under construction, and return to the same point.

Nearing completion, the building, designed with a rustic exterior to fit into the landscape, will provide rest rooms and space for lectures and classes in ecology.

ERNA NIXON PARK is not yet open to the public, but James Vencill, director of District 5 Parks and Recreation, hopes an adequate stage of completion can be reached in two to three weeks to allow the first group tours. They will be guided by members of the Junior Service League which has contributed $20,000 to the park's development.

Future plans call for extension of the present boardwalk by another 2,500 feet, and the addition of a building to house a herbarium, a library and dioramas.

TO DATE, EXPENDITURES on the park, a major effort to preserve what Mrs. Erna Nixon contends is the last remaining undisturbed hammock in the county, include the $156,000 purchase price, which utilized a $100,000 grant from the Florida Department of Natural Resources, the Service League contributions and a $17,500 Florida Bicentennial Commission Grant.

The purchase came about through the urging of Mrs. Nixon, a former biology teacher and naturalist from Chicago who came to Brevard in 1955. She began conducting tours through the hammock for school

children more than 20 years ago.

Picnic facilities will be made available near the parking lot. To protect the hammock's ecology, no picnicking will be allowed along the trail and boardwalk.

FIT ecology students along boardwalk

Mark Losey/Sentinel Star

Erna Nixon showing something of interest in the Hammock, to my mother and Grandfather.

ERNA NIXON PARK
1200 Evans Road
Melbourne, Florida